ICAROMENIPPUS AN AERIAL EXPEDITION

Menippus and a Friend

Edited by Gregory Zorzos

LUCIAN

Lucian was born in Samosata, Commage, Syria. Most of what we know about Lucian's life is derived from his own writings, which cannot always be taken at face value.

However, in *My Dream* Lucian tells that he was apprenticed to his uncle, a stonecutter, after he had stopped going to school. Lucian had shown some talent in modelling cows, horses, and human figures from wax. The apprenticeship lasted one day because he managed to break a slab with his chisel.

Lucian of Samosata lived under the Roman Emperors Antoninus Pius, M. Aurelius and Lucius Verus, Commodus, and perhaps Pertinax.

His mother-tongue was probably Aramaic, but as a young man he spent some years in Ionian, acquiring a Greek literary education. He also studied rhetoric and wandered through western Asia as a traveling lecturer.

ICAROMENIPPUS
AN AERIAL EXPEDITION
Menippus and a Friend

Menippus. Let me see, now.
First stage, Earth to Moon, 350 miles.
Second stage, up to the Sun, 500 leagues.
Then the third, to the actual Heaven and Zeus's citadel, might be put at a day's journey for an eagle in light marching order.

Friend. In the name of goodness, Menippus, what are these astronomical sums you are doing under your breath?
I have been dogging yon for some time, listening to your suns and moons, queerly mixed up with common earthly stages and leagues.

Menippus. Ah, you must not be surprised if my talk is rather exalted and ethereal;
I was making out the mileage of my journey.

Friend. Oh, I see; using stars to steer by, like the Phoenicians?

Menippus. Oh no, travelling among them.

Friend. Well, to be sure, it must have been a longish dream, if you lost yourself in it for whole leagues.

Menippus. Dream, my good man?
I am just come straight from Zeus.
Dream, indeed!

Friend. How?
What?
Our Menippus a literal godsend from Heaven?

Menippus. 'Tis even so; from very Zeus I come this day, eyes and ears yet full of wonders.
Oh, doubt, if you will.
That my fortune should pass belief makes it only the more gratifying.

Friend. Nay, my worshipful Olympian, how should I, 'a man begotten, treading this poor earth,' doubt him who transcends the clouds, a 'denizen of Heaven,' as Homer says?
But vouchsafe to tell me how you were uplifted, and where you got your mighty tall ladder.
There is hardly enough of Ganymede in your looks to suggest that you were carried off by the eagle for a cupbearer.

Menippus. I see you are bent on making a jest of it.
Well, it *is* extraordinary;
you could not be expected to see that it is not a romance.
The fact is, I needed neither ladder nor amorous eagle;
I had wings of my own.

Friend. Stranger and stranger!
This beats Daedalus.
What, you turned into a hawk or a crow on the sly?

Menippus. Now that is not a bad shot;
it was Daedalus's wing trick that I tried.

Friend. Well, talk of foolhardiness!
Did you like the idea of falling into the sea, and giving us a *Mare Menippeum* after the precedent of the *Icarium*?

Menippus. No fear.
Icarus's feathers were fastened with wax, and of course, directly the sun warmed this, he moulted and fell.
No wax for me, thank you.

Friend. How did you manage, then?
I declare I shall be believing you soon, if you go on like this.

Menippus. Well, I caught a fine eagle, and also a particularly powerful vulture, and cut off their wings above the shoulder-joint. . . .
But no; if you are not in a hurry, I may as well give you the enterprise from the beginning.

Friend. Do, do;
I am rapt aloft by your words already, my mouth open for your *bonne bouche*; as you love me, leave me not in those upper regions hung up by the ears!

Menippus. Listen, then;
it would be a sorry sight, a friend deserted, with his mouth open, and *sus per aures*.

- Well, a very short survey of life had convinced me of the absurdity and meanness and insecurity that pervade all human objects, such as wealth, office, power.
I was filled with contempt for them, realized that to care for them was to lose all chance of what deserved care, and determined to grovel no more, but fix my gaze upon the great All.
Here I found my first problem in what wise men call the universal order;
I could not tell how it came into being, who made it, what was its beginning, or what its end.
But my next step, which was the examination of details, landed me in yet worse perplexity.
I found the stars dotted quite casually about the sky, and I wanted to know what the sun was.
Especially the phenomena of the moon struck me as extraordinary, and quite passed my comprehension;
there must be some mystery to account for those many phases, I conjectured.
Nor could I feel any greater certainty about such things as the passage of lightning, the roll of thunder, the descent of rain and snow and hail.
In this state of mind, the best I could think of was to get at the truth of it all from the people called philosophers;
they of course would be able to give it

Menippus. So I selected the best of them, if solemnity of visage, pallor of complexion and length of beard are any criterion - for there could not be a moment's doubt of their soaring words and heaven-high thoughts - and in their hands I placed myself.

For a considerable sum down, and more to be paid when they should have perfected me in wisdom, I was to be made an airy metaphysician and instructed in the order of the universe.
Unfortunately, so far from dispelling my previous ignorance, they perplexed me more and more, with their daily drenches of beginnings and ends, atoms and voids, matters and forms.
My greatest difficulty was that, though they differed among themselves, and all they said was full of inconsistency and contradiction, they expected me to believe them, each pulling me in his own direction.

Friend. How absurd that wise men should quarrel about facts, and hold different opinions on the same things!

Menippus. Ah, but keep your laughter till you have heard something of their pretentious mystifications.
To begin with, their feet are on the ground; they are no taller than the rest of us 'men that walk the earth'; they are no sharper-sighted than their neighbours, some of them purblind, indeed, with age or indolence; and yet they say they can distinguish the limits of the sky, they measure the sun's circumference, take their walks in the supra-lunar regions, and specify the sizes and shapes of the stars as though they had fallen from them; often one of them could not tell you correctly the number of miles from Megara to Athens, but has no hesitation about the distance in feet from the sun to the moon.
How high the atmosphere is, how deep the sea, how far it is round the earth - they have the figures for all

that; and moreover, they have only to draw some circles, arrange a few triangles and squares, add certain complicated spheres, and lo, they have the cubic contents of Heaven.
Then, how reasonable and modest of them, dealing with subjects so debatable, to issue their views without a hint of uncertainty; thus it must be and it shall be; *contra gentes* they will have it so; they will tell you on oath the sun is a molten mass, the moon inhabited, and the stars water-drinkers, moisture being drawn up by the sun's rope and bucket and equitably distributed among them.
How their theories conflict is soon apparent; next-door neighbours?
no, they are miles apart.
In the first place, their views of the world differ.
Some say it had no beginning, and cannot end; others boldly talk of its creator and his procedure; what particularly entertained me was that these latter set up a contriver of the universe, but fail to mention where he came from, or what he stood on while about his elaborate task, though it is by no means obvious how there could be place or time before the universe came into being.

Friend. You really do make them out very audacious conjurers.

Menippus. My dear fellow, I wish I could give you their lucubrations on ideas and incorporeals, on finite and infinite.
Over that point, now, there is fierce battle; some circumscribe the All, others will have it unlimited.

At the same time they declare for a plurality of worlds, and speak scornfully of others who make only one.
And there is a bellicose person who maintains that war is the father of the universe 1.
As to Gods, I need hardly deal with that question.
For some of them God is a number; some swear by dogs and geese and plane-trees 2.
Some again banish all other Gods, and attribute the control of the universe to a single one; I got rather depressed on learning how small the supply of divinity was.
But I was comforted by the lavish souls who not only make many, but classify; there was a First God, and second and third classes of divinity.
Yet again, some regard the divine nature as unsubstantial and without form, while others conceive it as a substance.
Then they were not all disposed to recognize a Providence; some relieve the Gods of all care, as we relieve the superannuated of their civic duties; in fact, they treat them exactly like supernumeraries on the stage.
The last step is also taken, of saying that Gods do not exist at all, and leaving the world to drift along without a master or a guiding hand.
Well, when I heard all this, I dared not disbelieve people whose voices and beards were equally suggestive of Zeus.
But I knew not where to turn for a theory that was not open to exception, nor combated by one as soon as propounded by another.

I found myself in the state Homer has described; many a time I would vigorously start believing one of these gentlemen;
But then came second thoughts.
So in my distress I began to despair of ever getting any knowledge about these things on earth; the only possible escape from perplexity would be to take to myself wings and go up to Heaven.
Partly the wish was father to the thought; but it was confirmed by Aesop's Fables, from which it appears that Heaven is accessible to eagles, beetles, and sometimes camels.
It was pretty clear that I could not possibly develop feathers of my own.
But if I were to wear vulture's or eagle's wings - the only kinds equal to a man's weight - I might perhaps succeed.
I caught the birds, and effectually amputated the eagle's right, and the vulture's left wing.
These I fastened together, attached them to my shoulders with broad thick straps, and provided grips for my hands near the end of the quill-feathers.
Then I made experiments, first jumping up and helping the jump by flapping my hands, or imitating the way a goose raises itself without leaving the ground and combines running with flight.
Finding the machine obedient, I next made a bolder venture, went up the Acropolis, and launched myself from the cliff right over the theatre.
Getting safely to the bottom that time, my aspirations shot up aloft.

I took to starting from Parnes or Hymettus, flying to Geranea, thence to the top of the Acrocorinthus, and over Pholöe and Erymanthus to Taÿgetus.
The training for my venture was now complete; my powers were developed, and equal to a lofty flight; no more fledgeling essays for Menippus.
I went up Olympus, provisioning myself as lightly as possible.
The moment was come; I soared skywards, giddy at first with that great void below, but soon conquering this difficulty.
When I approached the Moon, long after parting from the clouds, I was conscious of fatigue, especially in the left or vulture's wing.
So I alighted and sat down to rest, having a bird's-eye view of the Earth, like the Homeric Zeus, Surveying now the Thracian horsemen's land, Now Mysia, and again, as the fancy took me, Greece or Persia or India.
From all which I drew a manifold delight.

Friend. Oh well, Menippus, tell me all about it.
I do not want to miss a single one of your travel experiences; if you picked up any stray information, let me have that too.
I promise myself a great many facts about the shape of the Earth, and how everything on it looked to you from your point of vantage.

Menippus. And you will not be disappointed there, friend. So do your best to get up to the Moon, with my story for travelling companion and showman of the terrestrial scene.

Imagine yourself first descrying a tiny Earth, far smaller than the Moon looks; on turning my eyes down, I could not think for some time what had become of our mighty mountains and vast sea.
If I had not caught sight of the Colossus of Rhodes and the Pharus tower, I assure you I should never have made out the Earth at all.
But their height and projection, with the faint shimmer of Ocean in the sun, showed me it must be the Earth I was looking at.
Then, when once I had got my sight properly focused, the whole human race was clear to me, not merely in the shape of nations and cities, but the individuals, sailing, fighting, ploughing, going to law; the women, the beasts, and in short every breed 'that feedeth on earth's foison.'

Friend. Most unconvincing and contradictory.
Just now you were searching for the Earth, it was so diminished by distance, and if the Colossus had not betrayed it, you would have taken it for something else; and now you develop suddenly into a Lynceus, and distinguish everything upon it, the men, the beasts, one might almost say the gnat-swarms. Explain, please.

Menippus. Why, to be sure! how did I come to leave out so essential a particular?
I had made out the Earth, you see, but could not distinguish any details; the distance was so great, quite beyond the scope of my vision; so I was much chagrined and baffled.

At this moment of depression - I was very near tears - who should come up behind me but Empedocles the physicist?
His complexion was like charcoal variegated with ashes, as if he had been baked.
I will not deny that I felt some tremors at the sight of him, taking him for some lunar spirit. But he said: 'Do not be afraid, Menippus;
A mortal I, no God; how vain thy dreams.
I am Empedocles the physicist. When I threw myself into the crater in such a hurry, the smoke of Etna whirled me off up here; and now I live in the Moon, doing a good deal of high thinking on a diet of dew.
So I have come to help you out of your difficulty; you are distressed, I take it, at not being able to see everything on the Earth.' 'Thank you so much, you good Empedocles,' I said; 'as soon as my wings have brought me back to Greece, I will remember to pour libations to you up the chimney, and salute you on the first of every month with three moonward yawns.' 'Endymion be my witness,' he replied, 'I had no thought of such a bargain; I was touched by the sight of your distress.
Now, what do you think is the way to sharpen your sight?'
'I have no idea, unless you were to remove the mist from my eyes for me; the sight seems quite bleared.'
'Oh, you can do without me; the thing that gives sharp sight you have brought with you from Earth.' 'Unconsciously, then; what is it?' 'Why, you know that you have on an eagle's right wing?' 'Of course I do; but what have wings and eyes to do with one another?' 'Only this,' he said; 'the eagle is far the

strongest-eyed of all living things, the only one that can look straight at the sun; the test of the true royal eagle is, his meeting its rays without blinking.'
'So I have heard; I wish I had taken out my own eyes when I was starting, and substituted the eagle's. I am an imperfect specimen now I am here, not up to the royal standard at all, but like the rejected bastards.'
'Well, you can very soon acquire one royal eye. If you will stand up for a minute, keep the vulture wing still, and work the other, your right eye, corresponding to that wing, will gain strength.
As for the other, its dimness cannot possibly be obviated, as it belongs to the inferior member.' 'Oh, I shall be quite content with aquiline vision for the right eye only,' I said; 'I have often observed that carpenters in ruling their wood find one better than two.'
So saying, I proceeded to carry out my instructions at once. Empedocles began gradually to disappear, and at last vanished in smoke.
I had no sooner flapped the wing than a flood of light enveloped me, and things that before I had not even been aware of became perfectly clear.
I turned my eyes down earthwards, and with ease discerned cities, men, and all that was going on, not merely in the open, but in the fancied security of houses.
There was Ptolemy in his sister's arms, the son of Lysimachus plotting against his father, Seleucus's son Antiochus making signs to his step-mother Stratonice, Alexander of Pherae being murdered by his wife, Antigonus corrupting his daughter-in-law, the son of Attalus putting the poison in his cup; Arsaces was in

the act of slaying his mistress, while the eunuch Arbaces drew his sword upon him; the guards were dragging Spatinus the Mede out from the banquet by the foot, with the lump on his brow from the golden cup.
Similar sights were to be seen in the palaces of Libya and Scythia and Thrace - adulteries, murders, treasons, robberies, perjuries, suspicions, and monstrous betrayals.
Such was the entertainment afforded me by royalty; private life was much more amusing; for I could make that out too. I saw Hermodorus the Epicurean perjuring himself for 40 mnas, Agathocles the Stoic suing a pupil for his fees, lawyer Clinias stealing a bowl from the temple of Asclepius, and Herophilus the cynic sleeping in a brothel.
Not to mention the multitude of burglars, litigants, usurers, duns; oh, it was a fine representative show!

Friend. I must say, Menippus, I should have liked the details here too; it all seems to have been very much to your taste.

Menippus. I could not go through the whole of it, even to please you; to take it in with the eyes kept one busy. But the main divisions were very much what Homer gives from the shield of Achilles: here junketings and marriages, there courts and councils, in another compartment a sacrifice, and hard by a mourning.
If I glanced at Getica, I would see the Getae at war; at Scythia, there were the Scythians wandering about on their waggons; half a turn in another direction gave

me Egyptians at the plough, or Phoenicians chaffering, Cilician pirates, Spartan flagellants, Athenians at law. All this was simultaneous, you understand; and you must try to conceive what a queer jumble it all made. It was as if a man were to collect a number of choristers, or rather of choruses 1, and then tell each individual to disregard the others and start a strain of his own; if each did his best, went his own way, and tried to drown his neighbour, can you imagine what the musical effect would be?

Friend. A very ridiculous confusion.

Menippus. Well, friend, such are the earthly dancers; the life of man is just such a discordant performance; not only are the voices jangled, but the steps are not uniform, the motions not concerted, the objects not agreed upon - until the impresario dismisses them one by one from the stage, with a 'not wanted.'
Then they are all alike, and quiet enough, confounding no longer their undisciplined rival strains. But as long as the show lasts in its marvellous diversity, there is plenty of food for laughter in its vagaries.
The people who most amused me, however, were those who dispute about boundaries, or pride themselves on cultivating the plain of Sicyon, or holding the Oenoë side of Marathon, or a thousand acres at Acharnae.
The whole of Greece, as I then saw it, might measure some four inches; how much smaller Athens on the same scale.
So I realized what sort of sized basis for their pride remains to our rich men.

The widest-acred of them all, methought, was the proud cultivator of an Epicurean atom.
Then I looked at the Peloponnese, my eyes fell on the Cynurian district, and the thought occurred that it was for this little plot, no broader than an Egyptian lentil, that all those Argives and Spartans fell in a single day.
Or if I saw a man puffed up by the possession of seven or eight
gold rings and half as many gold cups, again my lungs would begin to crow; why, Pangaeus with all its mines was about the size of a grain of millet.

Friend. You lucky man! what a rare sight you had! And how big, now, did the towns and the people look from there?

Menippus. You must often have seen a community of ants, some of them a seething mass, some going abroad, others coming back to town.
One is a scavenger, another a bustling porter loaded with a bit of bean-pod or half a wheat grain.
They no doubt have, on their modest myrmecic scale, their architects and politicians, their magistrates and composers and philosophers.
At any rate, what men and cities suggested to me was just so many ant-hills.
If you think the similitude too disparaging, look into the Thessalian legends, and you will find that the most warlike tribe there was the Myrmidons, or ants turned men.
Well, when I had had enough of contemplation and laughter, I roused myself and soared
To join the Gods, where dwells the Lord of storms.

I had only flown a couple of hundred yards, when Selene's feminine voice reached me: 'Menippus, do me an errand to Zeus, and I will wish you a pleasant journey.' 'You have only to name it,' I said, 'provided it is not something to carry.' 'It is a simple message of entreaty to Zeus. I am tired to death, you must know, of being slandered by these philosophers; they have no better occupation than impertinent curiosity about me - What am I? how big am I? why am I halved? why am I gibbous? I am inhabited; I am just a mirror hung over the sea; I am - whatever their latest fancy suggests. It is the last straw when they say my light is stolen, sham, imported from the sun, and keep on doing their best to get up jealousy and ill feeling between brother and sister.

They might have been contented with making *him* out a stone or a red-hot lump.

'These gentry who in the day look so stern and manly, dress so gravely, and are so revered by common men, would be surprised to learn how much I know of their vile nightly abominations.

I see them all, though I never tell; it would be too indecent to make revelations, and show up the contrast between their nightly doings and their public performances; so, if I catch one of them in adultery or theft or other nocturnal adventure, I pull my cloud veil over me; I do not want the vulgar to see old men disgracing their long beards and their virtuous calling.

But they go on giving tongue and worrying me all the same, and, so help me Night, I have thought many a time of going a long, long way off, out of reach of their impertinent tongues.

Will you remember to tell Zeus all this? and you may add that I cannot remain at my post unless he will pulverize the physicists, muzzle the logicians, raze the Porch, burn the Academy, and put an end to strolling in the Lyceum.
That might secure me a little peace from these daily mensurations.'
'I will remember,' said I, and resumed my upward flight to Heaven, through
A region where nor ox nor man had wrought.
For the Moon was soon but a small object, with the Earth entirely hidden behind it.
Three days' flight through the stars, with the Sun on my right hand, brought me close to Heaven; and my first idea was to go straight in as I was;
I should easily pass unobserved in virtue of my half-eagleship; for of course the eagle was Zeus's familiar; on second thoughts, though, my vulture wing would very soon betray Menippus.
So, thinking it better not to run any risks, I went up to the door and knocked. Hermes opened, took my name, and hurried off to inform Zeus.
After a brief wait I was asked to step in; I was now trembling with apprehension, and I found that the Gods, who were all seated together, were not quite easy themselves.
The unexpected nature of the visit was slightly disturbing to them, and they had visions of all mankind arriving at my heels by the same conveyance.
But Zeus bent upon me a Titanic glance, awful, penetrating, and spoke:
Who art thou?
where thy city?

who thy kin?
At the sound, I nearly died of fear, but remained upright, though mute and paralysed by that thunderous voice.
I gradually recovered, began at the beginning, and gave a clear account of myself - how I had been possessed with curiosity about the heavens, had gone to the philosophers, found their accounts conflicting, and grown tired of being logically rent in twain; so I came to my great idea, my wings, and ultimately to Heaven; I added Selene's message.
Zeus smiled and slightly unbent his brow. 'What of Otus and Ephialtes now?' he said; 'here is Menippus scaling Heaven! Well, well, for to-day consider yourself our guest.
Tomorrow we will treat with you of your business, and send you on your way.' And therewith he rose and walked to the acoustic centre of Heaven, it being prayer time.
As he went, he put questions to me about earthly affairs, beginning with, What was wheat a quarter in Greece? had we suffered much from cold last winter?
and did the vegetables want more rain? Then he wished to know whether any of Phidias's kin were alive, why there had been no Diasia at Athens all these years, whether his Olympieum was ever going to be completed, and had the robbers of his temple at Dodona been caught?
I answered all these questions, and he proceeded: - 'Tell me, Menippus, what are men's feelings towards me?' 'What should they be, Lord, but those of absolute reverence, as to the King of all Gods?' 'Now, now,

chaffing as usual,' he said; 'I know their fickleness very well, for all your dissimulation.
There was a time when I was their prophet, their healer, and their all,
And Zeus filled every street and gathering-place.
In those days Dodona and Pisa were glorious and far-famed, and I could not get a view for the clouds of sacrificial steam.
But now Apollo has set up his oracle at Delphi, Asclepius his temple of health at Pergamum, Bendis and Anubis and Artemis their shrines in Thrace, Egypt, Ephesus; and to these all run; theirs the festal gatherings and the hecatombs.
As for me, I am superannuated; they think themselves very generous if they offer me a victim at Olympia at four-year intervals. My altars are cold as Plato's *Laws* or Chrysippus's *Syllogisms*.'
So talking, we reached the spot where he was to sit and listen to the prayers.
There was a row of openings with lids like well-covers, and a chair of gold by each. Zeus took his seat at the first, lifted off the lid and inclined his ear.
From every quarter of Earth were coming the most various and contradictory petitions; for I too bent down my head and listened. Here are specimens. 'O Zeus, that I might be king!' 'O Zeus, that my onions and garlic might thrive!' 'Ye Gods, a speedy death for my father!' Or again, 'Would that I might succeed to my wife's property!' 'Grant that my plot against my brother be not detected.' 'Let me win my suit.' 'Give me an Olympic garland.'
Of those at sea, one prayed for a north, another for a south wind; the farmer asked for rain, the fuller for

sun. Zeus listened, and gave each prayer careful consideration, but without promising to grant them all;
Our Father this bestowed, and that withheld.
Righteous prayers he allowed to come up through the hole, received and laid them down at his right, while he sent the unholy ones packing with a downward puff of breath, that Heaven might not be defiled by their entrance. In one case
I saw him puzzled; two men praying for opposite things and promising the same sacrifices, he could not tell which of them to favour, and experienced a truly Academic suspense of judgement, showing a reserve and equilibrium worthy of Pyrrho himself.
The prayers disposed of, he went on to the next chair and opening, and attended to oaths and their takers.
These done with, and Hermodorus the Epicurean annihilated, he proceeded to the next chair to deal with omens, prophetic voices, and auguries.
Then came the turn of the sacrifice aperture, through which the smoke came up and communicated to Zeus the name of the devotee it represented.
After that, he was free to give his wind and weather orders: - Rain for Scythia to-day, a thunderstorm for Libya, snow for Greece. The north wind he instructed to blow in Lydia, the west to raise a storm in the Adriatic, the south to take a rest; a thousand bushels of hail to be distributed over Cappadocia.
His work was now pretty well completed, and as it was just dinner time, we went to the banquet hall.
Hermes received me, and gave me my place next to a group of Gods whose alien origin left them in a rather doubtful position - Pan, the Corybants, Attis, and Sabazius.

I was supplied with bread by Demeter, wine by Dionysus, meat by Heracles, myrtle-blossoms by Aphrodite, and sprats by Posidon.
But I also got a sly taste of ambrosia and nectar; good-natured Ganymede, as often as he saw that Zeus's attention was engaged elsewhere, brought round the nectar and indulged me with a half-pint or so.
The Gods, as Homer (who I think must have had the same opportunities of observation as myself) somewhere says, neither eat bread nor drink the ruddy wine; they heap their plates with ambrosia, and are nectar-bibbers; but their choicest dainties are the smoke of sacrifice ascending with rich fumes, and the blood of victims poured by their worshippers round the altars.
During dinner, Apollo harped, Silenus danced his wild measures, the Muses uprose and sang to us from Hesiod's *Birth of Gods*, and the first of Pindar's odes.
When we had our fill and had well drunken, we slumbered, each where he was.
Slept all the Gods, and men with plumed helms,
That livelong night; but me kind sleep forsook;
for I had much upon my mind; most of all, how came it that Apollo, in all that time, had never grown a beard?
and how was night possible in Heaven, with the sun always there taking his share of the good cheer?
So I had but a short nap of it. And in the morning Zeus arose, and bade summon an assembly.
When all were gathered, he thus commenced: - 'The immediate occasion of my summoning you is the arrival of this stranger yesterday.

But I have long intended to take counsel with you regarding the philosophers, and now, urged by Selene and her complaints, I have determined to defer the consideration of the question no longer.
There is a class which has recently become conspicuous among men; they are idle, quarrelsome, vain, irritable, lickerish, silly, puffed up, arrogant, and, in Homeric phrase, vain cumberers of the earth.
These men have divided themselves into bands, each dwelling in a separate word-maze of its own construction, and call themselves Stoics, Epicureans, Peripatetics, and more farcical names yet.
Then they take to themselves the holy name of Virtue, and with uplifted brows and flowing beards exhibit the deceitful semblance that hides immoral lives; their model is the tragic actor, from whom if you strip off the mask and the gold-spangled robe, there is nothing left but a paltry fellow hired for a few shillings to play a part.
'Nevertheless, quite undeterred by their own characters, they scorn the human and travesty the divine; they gather a company of guileless youths, and feed them with solemn chatter upon Virtue and quibbling verbal puzzles; in their pupils' presence they are all for fortitude and temperance, and have no words bad enough for wealth and pleasure: when they are by themselves, there is no limit to their gluttony, their lechery, their licking of dirty pence. But the head and front of their offending is this: they neither work themselves nor help others' work; they are useless drones, Of no avail in council nor in war;
which notwithstanding, they censure others; they store up poisoned words, they con invectives, they heap

their neighbours with reproaches; their highest honours are for him who shall be loudest and most overbearing and boldest in abuse.

'Ask one of these brawling bawling censors, And what do *you* do? in God's name, what shall we call *your* contribution to progress? and he would reply, if conscience and truth were anything to him: I consider it superfluous to sail the sea or till the earth or fight for my country or follow a trade; but I have a loud voice and a dirty body; I eschew warm water and go barefoot through the winter; I am a Momus who can always pick holes in other people's coats; if a rich man keeps a costly table or a mistress, I make it my business to be properly horrified; but if my familiar friend is lying sick, in need of help and care, I am not aware of it. Such, your Godheads, is the nature of this vermin.

'There is a special insolence in those who call themselves Epicureans; these go so far as to lay their hands on our character; we take no interest in human affairs, they say, and in fact have nothing to do with the course of events.

And this is a serious question for you; if once they infect their generation with this view, you will learn what hunger means. Who will sacrifice to you, if he does not expect to profit by it?

As to Selene's complaints, you all heard them yesterday from this stranger's lips. And now decide upon such measures as shall advantage mankind and secure your own safety.'

Zeus had no sooner closed his speech than clamour prevailed, all crying at once: Blast! burn! annihilate! to the pit with them! to Tartarus! to the Giants!

Zeus ordered silence again, and then, 'Your wishes,' he said, 'shall be executed; they shall all be annihilated, and their logic with them.
But just at present chastisement is not lawful; you are aware that we are now in the four months of the long vacation; the formal notice has lately been issued.
In the spring of next year, the baleful levin-bolt shall give them the fate they deserve.'
He spake, and sealed his word with lowering brows.
'As to Menippus,' he added, 'my pleasure is this. He shall be deprived of his wings, and so incapacitated for repeating his visit, but shall to-day be conveyed back to Earth by Hermes.' So saying, he dismissed the assembly.
The Cyllenian accordingly lifted me up by the right ear, and yesterday evening deposited me in the Ceramicus.
And now, friend, you have all the latest from Heaven. I must be off to the Poecile, to let the philosophers loitering there know the luck they are in.

H.

Footnotes

130:1 Variously attributed to Heraclitus, who denies the possibility of repose, and insists that all things are in a state of flux; and to Empedocles, who makes all change and becoming depend on the interaction of the two principles, attraction and repulsion.

130:2 Socrates made a practice of substituting these for the names of Gods in his oaths.

136:1 The Greek chorus combined singing with dancing.

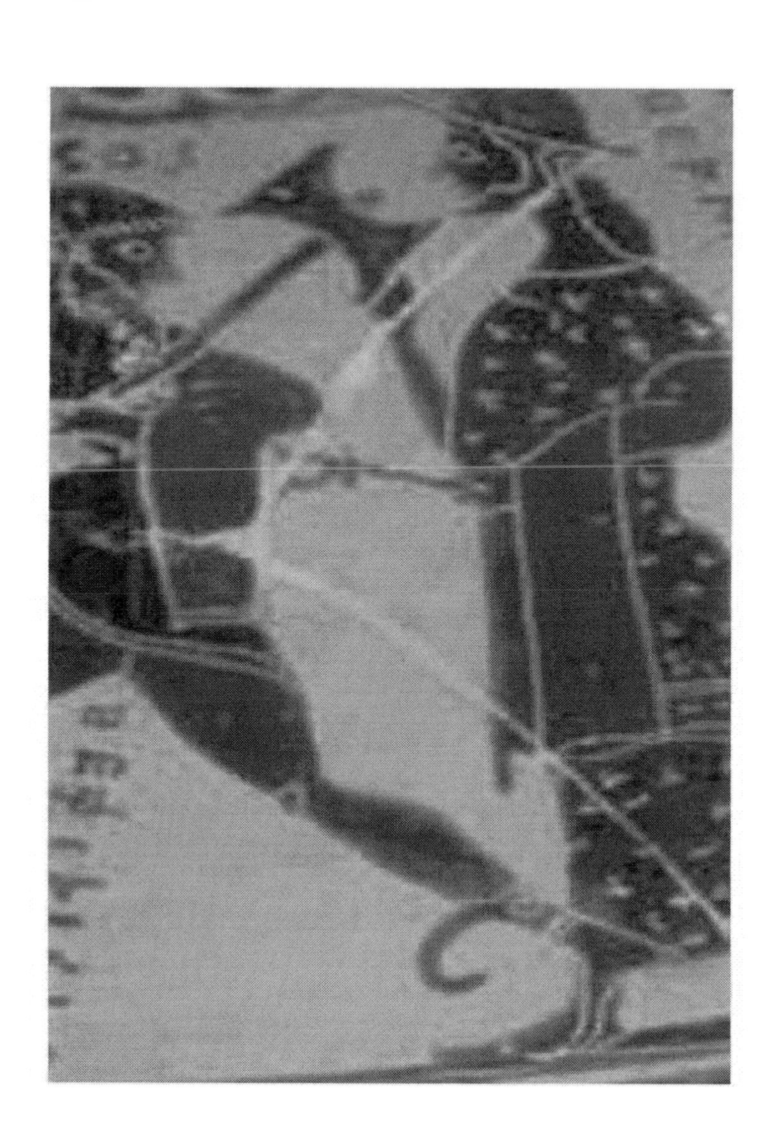